I Can Be a Shopkeeper

يمكنني أن أصبح بائعًا

By KR Clarry

Illustrated by John Robert Azuelo

Please note, the two versions of this story have been written to be as close as possible. However, in some cases they differ to accommodate the nuances of each language.

برجاء ملاحظة أن نسختَي هذه القصة تمت كتابتهما لتكونا متقاربتين قدر الإمكان. لكن قد تكون هناك أحيانًا بعض الاختلافات لتناسب كل لغة.

Library For All Ltd.

2

These are shopkeepers.

هؤلاء بائعون.

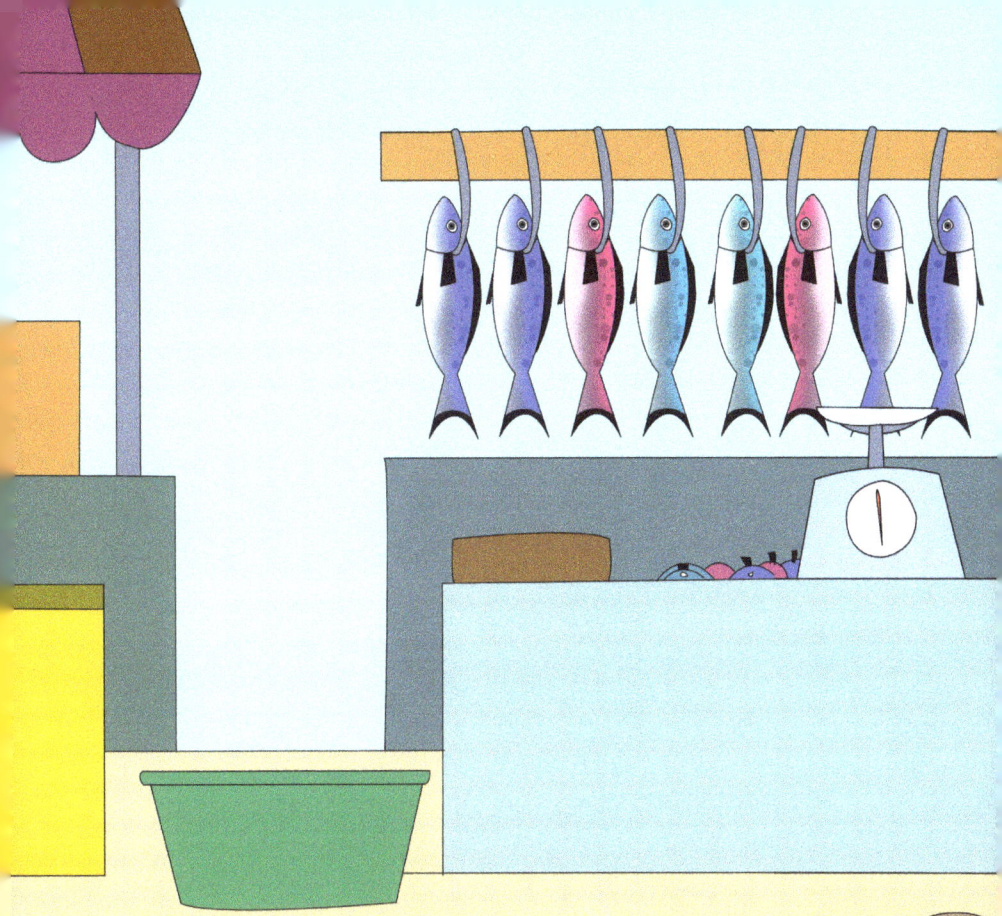

They work in shops.

إنهم يعملون في المتاجر.

Shopkeepers sell many different
items to customers.

يبيع البائعون العديد من السلع
المختلفة للزبائن.

Shopkeepers use shelves to
display what can be bought
and cash registers to
organise money.

البائعون يستخدمون الأرفف
لعرض ما يمكن شراؤه وماكينات
تسجيل النقدية لتنظيم النقود.

They can sell food, drinks, clothes,
shoes, toys, books and furniture.

يمكنهم بيع الطعام والمشروبات والملابس
والأحذية والألعاب والكتب والأثاث.

There are special shopkeepers that
sell flowers, bread, medicine or
electrical products.

هناك بائعون متخصصون لبيع الزهور أو
الخبز أو الأدوية أو السلع الكهربائية.

There are shopkeepers all
around the world.

هناك بائعون في كل مكان بالعالم.

I can learn to be a shopkeeper by studying business at college or university.

يمكنني أن أتعلم أن أعمل بائعًا عن طريق دراسة الأعمال في الكلية أو الجامعة.

Then I can help my community buy
the things they need to live well.

ثمَ يمكنني أن أساعد أفراد مجتمعي لشراء
الأشياء التي يحتاجونها لعيش حياة جيدة.

You can use these questions to talk about this book with your family, friends and teachers.

What did you learn from this book?

Describe this book in one word. Funny? Scary? Colourful? Interesting?

How did this book make you feel when you finished reading it?

What was your favourite part of this book?

About the author

KR Clarry grew up with a passion for reading, writing and learning. As a teacher, aka Miss Clarry, she shares the love of lifelong learning with the next generation. KR enjoys bringing stories alive through modelled and shared reading and writing experiences as well as through visual art, dance, music, multimedia and drama activities.

KR's ultimate goal is to make a positive difference in the world and works to inspire children to aim high to be the best versions of themselves that they can be.

"Be the change that you wish to see in the world."

~ Mahatma Gandhi.

"I alone cannot change the world, but I can cast a stone across the waters to create many ripples."

~ Mother Teresa.

Did you enjoy this book?

We have hundreds more expertly curated original stories to choose from.

We work in partnership with authors, educators, cultural advisors, governments and NGOs to bring the joy of reading to children everywhere.

Did you know?

We create global impact in these fields by embracing the United Nations Sustainable Development Goals.

libraryforall.org

Library For All is an Australian not for profit organisation with a mission to make knowledge accessible to all via an innovative digital library solution. Visit us at libraryforall.org

I Can Be a Shopkeeper

This edition published 2024

Published by Library For All Ltd
Email: info@libraryforall.org
URL: libraryforall.org

Original illustrations by John Robert Azuelo

I Can Be a Shopkeeper
Clarry, KR
ISBN: 978-1-923143-99-9
SKU04361

www.ingramcontent.com/pod-product-compliance
Lightning Source LLC
Chambersburg PA
CBHW042349040426
42448CB00019B/3475